the reckless kind

poetry for the
heartbroken
and healing

bella ryan

First Printing, 2020

ISBN: 9798651725113

to you,
even so

table of contents

prologue: halloween   2
bare-boned   5
ecdysis   6
him: rhubarb   7
(over)   8
do i believe in omens?   9
blue birds and bumble bees   10
shameful behavior   11
good intentions   12
hey benny   13
how our darkest hours shone   14
a mystery   16
self-doubt   17
the keyboard march   18
goodbye (?)   19
another poem about the mountains   20
a long drive   21
distant   22
romanticizing the rain   23
until dawn   24
ode to the empty   25
to the man on the moon   26
hunger these days   27
april (i)   28
fries with that   29
amazon   30
colorado soul   31
passive humanitarian   32
matthew 21:12   33
this pen has fortitude   34
solitary companion   35

new year (2019)	36
no new yorker	37
memory care	38
heartbreak (a pros & cons list)	40
here's the bittersweet twist	41
in a highway hotel	42
heirloom	43
luck of the irish	44
a self-care mantra	45
that time we tried again	46
cardiac	47
naturally disasterous	48
we always felt the same	49
confessions of a windy day	50
mountain-top dance	51
anthem of american adoration	52
leg day	54
on education	55
disobedience	56
chemistry	57
dark affairs	58
april (ii)	59
garden of gods	60
mercy	61
h & k	62
one step forward…	63
the day i resolved to forget yesterday	64
hey may	65
revelations	66
tidal lock	67
storm warning	68
rebirth	69
p.n.w.	70
summit	71
new age dreams	72

san franscico sourdough 73
moving (back) in 74
sweet-heart 75
somebody new 76
dear flat earth society 77
you are no adventurer 78
a little Faith 79
oasis 80
turtle dove 81
this body 82
impression, sunset 83
where hope lay 84

this story starts with a starving heart
and a love that wouldn't eat.

prologue: halloween

(oct. 1)
you are out hunting.
i make corned beef, your favorite,
cause i know you'll be bummed
that you didn't catch dinner

(oct. 2)
i take a bus with my best friend
to new york city. she's moving
away at the end of the month,
but tonight, we forget with
tequila and sour patch kids

(oct. 5)
i take you to the cider mill,
to show you the waterfall

(oct. 9)
you are in the hospital, so
i lecture you on taking care of yourself
because i intend to love you
for the next several decades

(oct. 13)
you fulfill your three-year promise to me
and finally take me apple picking
it rains and the fruit glistens and
you watch me in the way that
makes me fly

(oct. 16)
i make applesauce, no cinnamon,
just how you like it. more of your
coworkers want to commission my art,
so i paint; how lucky i am to be loved
by a man who thinks i'm
prettiest with a paintbrush

(oct. 18)
you have a twenty-four hour shift at work,
but we spend the day flirting and teasing

(oct. 20)
you're hunting again, so
i go out dancing with friends.
under the bar lights, lonely sway,
i wish you were here

(oct. 22)
we plan to buy a truck to drive
to colorado when we move
in a few months

(oct. 24)
you tell me you have the same feeling as before
i am helpless in the way i want to help you

(oct. 27)
from upstairs,
i text you an article about how
sex reduces depression,
i tell you that i'm feeling sad

(oct. 29)
it's late when you pick me up
you bring me chicken nuggets
"god, i'm so in love with you,"
i laugh, but you are quiet

(oct. 30)
another all-day-all-night shift,
i ask what to bring you for dinner
whatever, whenever, sounds good to me
i wake up in the middle of the night,
but you tell me to go back to bed and you don't
respond when i say i love you and i miss you

(oct. 31)
i come home and find you passed out on the couch,
empty wine bottle on the counter. i kiss your forehead,
but you don't stir. beside you, a folded note sits
like a broken-winged bird. secrets curl from it like
smoke wisps. it's not for me, but i still read it
and learn how words could hurt that much,
when they're about her and leaving me.

bare-boned

your grandmother told you the secret
to a long marriage was to never let
the other go to bed angry—so you told me,
as you tugged me from the couch
where i was playing mad, held me on top of you,
and wouldn't let me go until i was
red from laughing.

that was two years ago. if i could remember
the last time i went to sleep happy, i think
i'd be okay. god, this delirium has pinned me to
this bed and i haven't been hungry in days. . .
why do you keep listening to that same song
over and over and over? what i'd give to be
asleep again, but that's all i've been doing for
the last seventy-two on-and-off hours and
it might just melt me away. i wish it would.
i'd rather feel nothing than all this.

so since i can't remember that, i remember you—
all the ways you made me laugh,
all before you drove me mad

ecdysis

started at my collarbones & peeled you off in layers,
nails latched deep into my own pieces, molting,
raking the falsehood foliage over
that winter's frozen dirt

and if i wanted to get rid of you,
do i have to get rid of the me that you sculpted to life?

i try to recall her
but i take that off too
i won't be the girl who fell in love with you again

this raw skin burns
but it grows back thick

him: rhubarb

(the leaves)

overs

(the softest way to put what we do)

we love like a head on car collision
at 95 miles per beat of our hearts
metal fusing to metal
tooth and nail
fighting
skin

we love like july fourth fireworks
gunpowder set on fire and launched
in the percussion night sky
raining colored light
bursting
sound

we love like the deep sea ocean
pressure of ten thousand meters
breeding the uncharted
dark, fearless world
waltzing to
sonar

do i believe in omens?

well,
i was chased out of the grand canyon
by a screaming raven with a hairy beak,
on the way to my mother's wedding.
i was seven. i didn't know much,

it might have been augury
against love, heights, or arizona,
i'm still not sure

but ten years later,
when my single mother is afraid
of how high your love is taking me,
i told her you were worth the risk

love isn't blind, love is an optimistic skeptic.
stars spelled nothing but looked
pretty in your eyes, and
the only future i could read in your palms
was my own hope for your hands to hold
me so softly for the rest of my days

you were made up of warning signs
but all i could see was your smiles and
the way you made me dizzy (good dizzy)
i guess i was too naive to watch out
for anything but blackbirds

blue birds & bumble bees

we were never winter lovers,
but we took what we could get.

your little smirk as you asked
if i was cold (knowing damn well
we'd called on this blizzard ourselves)

even when our world had frozen over,
you kissed in all the right places
(i swear roses bloomed on my thighs
like the sunniest days)

this new garden grew bitter fruit
honeysuckles that stung the tongue,
thick-skinned strawberries
rotten-sweet on the inside

we drug each other to a wicked eden,
a starvation harvest, a lovely lie,
lounged in longing for any warmth at all
the skin of your back scratched to hell
by the thorns you plucked from me

shameful behavior

i wish i could say i was a strong woman
you know, the sort who would die before
dependence, kick-ass to anyone who
even smells of shit, and definitely
would have been gone by now.

yeah, no—instead, i plead for you to
love me, even stone-hearted, even empty,
then bask in ravenous denial when you
refuse, then think i might win you
back with my quick-to-please mouth

remember, you were my first love, so i
never learned how to deal with someone
screwing me over like this, and it's starting
to look like grace and self-respect are
not my first instinct

i am furious and i am desperate.
i want to roundhouse hurl you off
the tallest mountain in this god-forsaken
heartbreak state and i want you to hold
me while i cry

to hell with me. i'm still in love with you.

good intentions

sloth is the measure time slows as
these silver sheets cling to our
limbs, begging us to reminisce
in that old-fashioned way that
makes us stay;
greed & *gluttony* are the sisters in
our eyes meeting that can never have
enough of how good more feels,
how i could never be sufficiently full
of you;
envy is why my fists ball in the blankets,
as they covet the duvet's pull around
your hips;
wrath is hidden in the blades of our
teeth, a push-and-pull-and-pin and
how i learn to love like a fighter,
bruised and grinning;
pride is a flavor of satisfaction that
melts on my lips, salty and warm,
a pleasure in performance;
and *lust* is queen bee, drizzled with
syrup and topped with a cherry

hey benny

i thought you thought you might make me feel better,
anesthetic for the angry & desperately apathetic
truth was, i trusted you more than i trusted myself
because i wasn't myself, you know, i mean, i thought
i'd forgotten about you until i was watching this
nature show about a fungus that gets into tiny ant
brains, leads them to high places, and eats them
inside-out.

all this to say, i might have forgiven you if you
hadn't done the same thing to her, too. all this to say,
you took my misery as a means for gratification
and you call *me* the liar? all this to say, you were better
before you grew up and decided that sad girls were
your favorite type of meal. whatever. you're all but
forgotten, besides bad dreams and metaphors. i didn't
want to write this, but i always tell the full story and i
don't think i've forgiven myself, either.

you're a shit friend.

how our darkest hours shone

heartbreak was a bitch—
a writhing globe of wasted years &
too many ugly, hungry hands &
you should have belonged to me &
only me, love

so i'll do the same to you, love
vengeful in the light of your crimes
and shameful in the shadows of mine
you've brought out the worst in me, love,
you've made me cold inside

i—
never knew i could hurt you this way, love
you did it to me first, love
i didn't think you cared

if you did then why'd you stray, love?
and why'd i do the same, love?
well, we're human and we're scared—
so now we feel the same, love,
i'd wish it all away, love. . .

even if we can't ignore
that ugly mess outside the door,
i've never seen you cry before—

even if it's over, stay,
we'll hold each other anyway
rest in all the pain we share
put off our own doomsday—

it's pretty, don't you think, love?
how slowly this ship sinks, love
we made this bed as one, love—
we'll burn it just the same.

a mystery

this perpetual exhaustion,
a bed-craving, daydreaming
about sleeping. my favorite
hobby is napping. they can call
me lazy, but my bones weigh
down my mind until
consciousness sinks me. hello,
adenosine, some old friend.
i'll just lay down for a moment.

self-doubt

on having faith:
how am i supposed
to believe in something
that keeps letting me down?

i'm talking about these feet,
which have led me here then
left me for dead, so i'm not
sure where to go but

these fists, which pound on
my own soul, seeking asylum,
but i have never been a refuge and

these tears, which paint me weak
in the voice and this mouth, which
can't decide where to call home for

these knees, which have only ever learned
how to pray to a god who has found
worship somewhere else.

have a little faith in yourself,
they say. i must be an atheist.

the keyboard march

my fingers are puppeteers.
men kneeling, necks bent in prayer,
stiff monks, struggling to wake

they're mine. my letters.
my voice when i have no voice,
my portal and passion and
they play such sweet homilies

i would know them blind,
tracing the trenches and
feeling the familiar
and

tap tap tap tap
i can find myself again
(at least before she hides again)

goodbye (?)

here's how i know you've changed me:
i am brave enough to ask you for a goodbye kiss
(selfish enough to want one more taste,
and/or foolish enough to think it won't fade)

we stand in our house, door wide open,
a sanctuary to the good memories
buried now by the bad

i tell you this *can't* be the last time, and
i have never been a good liar but it seems
you're rubbing off on me

please don't make me go. i'm not too proud to
beg for your heart but i know you're too proud
to give it back and you were supposed to be
my fairy tale, a happily ever after only ending
in twin graves and i'd forget everything wrong
right now, if you'd just let me

i'm stalling. if this is over, i don't know
what else i have left. love, you're my lighthouse.
don't make me count the times you've saved me.

in the rear-view mirror,
you smile with your eyes when you see me.
even still.

another poem
about the mountains

she said, desert girl,
dry skin, wet lips,
sunflower crown and
sandstorm smiles,
where have you run?

she said, the marshes rang,
the air like left-out
lemongrass tea,
wind-wisped hair,
but the water is too dark
too quiet

she said, the sea called,
sirens or venus or some
sweet spell, but the sand
was too soft and
the salt stung

tomorrow
i wander home

a long drive

a little gratitude to the girl
who drove me there,

so i could rest my head on the cold window,
watch the countryside sweep by,
wonder how many miles i was from you
(when will i stop thinking about you?)

she holds my hand. she sings, i cry,
but i might, maybe, be alright

she turns up the radio—*sing with me!*
i can't much say no, and we get lost
somewhere between nebraska and
never looking back

distant

again,
i'm stuck at the *and*
&
it feels like i am buried in the middle
of sentences that keep getting cut off,
&
i inhale,
&
half of my heart is across the world,
so suddenly,
i'm a tachycardic monologue,
i'm back to idealism and naps
because i don't think i can breathe
with this reality stuck in my throat
&
and,
and,
and

i wish i could just forget you.

romanticizing the rain

i tried
i tried to be the girl who
dances in puddles and
sticks out her tongue to catch
the drops and
yet
the
rain
still makes me cry,
like, stain the pillow
salt-water, heaving
heavy heart,
it just sounds so much like
drizzling loneliness but
it's nothing besides
the smell of a slippery cliff
and maybe
i'm just a sad girl,
and the rain is my excuse
because if the sky is crying,
then so must i

until dawn

i never say goodnight on the good days,
so that maybe it continues to tomorrow

this hasn't worked for the past two years,
but neither does anything else, and it keeps
getting harder to look toward tomorrow

and my biggest fear is that i've already been
the happiest i'll ever be, so all that is left
are dreams that are too easy to forget, and
what if i never move on to tomorrow?

i'd like to go back. i'd like to stay there.
i'm so tired of living for something that's
already gone, so i'll pray for the dusk to
be soft to a girl who doesn't want to move on
and maybe i'll say goodnight, tomorrow

ode to the empty

to the empty passenger seat,
the crater in this bed beside me,
the hollow in my hand:

sorry for the staring, see,
he used to make his home there—
right. . . there, and i can still
see him in this barren air

all at once, here again,
i can breathe again,
i can cry again,
i can—

this space is all that isn't gone,
a place to love these used-to-be's,
these vacant homes, these
lost, lorn shrines

to the man on the moon

i'm sorry for forgetting you,
which is to say,
i'm sorry for growing up,
for looking at you and seeing
your face turn to craters, to dust,
for realizing you were the unobtainable
and for shedding off my idealism like the
too-tight skin it was. for closing the
blinds when i sleep—you'll remember,
i used to be afraid of the dark, but now
it's the only way i can sleep. that's the thing,
you kept me up, and you never spoke.
you taught me silence, and i couldn't live
in silence any longer. the earth screams to
me now that i belong here, and i believe it.
you were the first man i fell in love with,
but i need more than crescent smiles and
someone who dims the sun

hunger these days

you'd taste good with banana bread
on a sunday morning,
two loves i haven't made in months—

the latter reminds me of you, i guess,
how you'd steal the chocolate chips
and leave no crumbs behind

i think about you too much
that my stomach aches like i've overindulged
but these days, i never eat enough
i've lost weight—but my love of you?
that stays like the bitter taste of coffee,
lukewarm and waiting,
needed and gone

april (i)

inevitable fool,
listened when they said
it never rains in april

forgot your coat
because you were too busy
admiring the grey skies

who thought petrichor
made a pretty poem

fries with that

can i get *uhhhhhhhh*
cheeseburger, without the cheese,
because it makes me think of cows,
and the cattle industry makes me sad.
i am not in the business of being sad.
i know i'm still asking for the meat,
but there's no such thing as a
bread and lettuce burger.
it's a common pattern in my life,
doing things half-way, so i might be
a horrible vegan, but i'm great optimist.
i tried knitting a sweater once but now
i only have a scarf. i'm all for bunking
with the stars but it would be nice to
reach the moon once. what i mean
to say is, how do i justify having a
finish line if i know i'll never reach it
what i mean to say is, i'm supposed to
be on a diet and i don't know why i'm
telling the drive-through voice-box this,
but, to be fair, you did ask how you could
help me today, so,
can i get a vanilla cone to take the edge off?

                              ma'am, the machine is—

i figured

amazons

war, distance, death, all
weaker than these air-tight
bonds between my girls and i.
my best friend promises me
more of herself than i know
of my own, and i'll defend her
from the gates of hell.
i've never been a fierce woman,
but i learned fury for her,
and the earth's knees shook
at the juxtaposition of our
joy and ire, how we smile
inward at each other then
turn with a snarl at the enemy.
there is life,
then there is friendship,
and the fight worth fighting.

colorado soul

they call it wanderlust,
i call it chasing florets
through mountaintops,
humming with the wind
which whistles dry grass,
an ache for the sunrise,
and the quiet friend
by a campfire.

passive humanitarian

on finding my *because*:
it was not under the bed,
where i hid. i thought i
felt it in the rain on my
neck, but that was just
water. i screamed at the
sky and the sky said
nothing because skies
don't talk back. i laid
laughing on the floor at midnight
trying to stimulate serotonin
and also i was slightly sleep
deprived. but i did know my
because, that i was meant to
help others, but how is that
possible when i cannot even
help myself? my socks don't
match. i want to tell the tired
mother at the store that her
shirt is on backwards but i
must be too shy. *yikes*, i
think. i think i care too
deeply for a self-proclaimed
stoic. i want to help.
i don't know how.

matthew 21:12

sunday school said,
your body is a temple;
it doesn't belong to you

but when you knelt there,
ripe in the gleam of such sweet worship,
how could i say no?
church doors don't lock,
and bad men don't pray

but i don't answer prayers, boy,
i can't collect the stars,
your incense burns more the longer you stay
the smoke gathers on my walls

you get tired of things i can't fix, and maybe
other gods will give you what you need

months pass, i'll clean up this mess,
take down the crosses and cover the altar
scrub your stains away
see, they were wrong, and you were wrong,
this is no holy place at all—

it's home,
it's mine, but still,
isn't it divine?

this pen has fortitude

it has my back, but
it's the insomniac, not me
pounding at my door
in the middle of the night,
a backwoods paul revere,
bringing that gift death gives us:
urgency—

i need to create before i can't,
you see. pull out the valve
and let off the pressure,
this pen is a defibrillator,
scrawling a lightning storm
in my heart, dilating my lungs
until they're ready to give birth
to this. to me. to me. to this.

solitary companion

my body rejects *lonely* like a failed transplant,
like my immune system knows it's a disease, and
needs an i.v. that holds my hand, and
rehydrates me after these months
of crying by myself.

see, "by myself" is culture shock and
i don't know this language. i don't know
why no one is here when they all
promised me better, okay?
give a girl a break, and maybe
a hug.

this *lonely* glows in the dark,
which i thought i was afraid of
until it was too bright to sleep
it's neon yellow, like street lights,
but the road is empty. it's empty.
people belong here—

this *lonely* doesn't belong here,
but it's the only company i've got,
you know. it's that roommate
who leaves dirty dishes in the sink,
forgets rent, and tries too hard
to be your friend

it keeps me here,
tells me it's safer, but
lonely is a liar

new year (2019)

i tip backwards over the staircase,
landing where i came from
but my old self isn't there to catch the fall

i said,
no kiss for me, knave

i'll rest my aches
in the bellies of friends
as our laughter carries me
over flat ground, for a bit

and i've stopped looking where i'm going,
hold on to where i've been,
and remember that
life persists

no new yorker

you buy return tickets to homes
we already built & wrecked
& expect me to feel salvation there,
as if i could find peace
where there is only exoskeletons left—
i shed that skin once,
and this new one needs mountains & pinecone pulses &
constant calluses & to never walk backwards

i'm making changes.
i want to be proud of me, not the things i give away,
i have solace in my own horizon
& shelter in my dreams
i will not trade high winds for ceiling fans,
or settle for places that aren't in my eyes

you had your chance. you had your chance.

memory care

i get a job in an alzheimer's unit.

harry asks me for a kiss again, so
i show him my ring that i can't seem
to take off

martie is pacing, always pacing,
worse by the day, but she pauses
for a hug

darryl's dancing on the dining room table,
norma is crying because she remembered
her husband is dead, again, and she thinks
it was only last week. lola relives her
hollywood days, wicked clever still

eddie likes to throw his cane at us
if we upset him—and, if i'm honest,
i dread bringing him to bed,
for all the fight he gives

tonight is no different, but i can't
be mad, you know, as he glares
when i ask for his glasses

every breath of his is tight and pained
i wish i could help him rest easier,
but instead, i show him an old picture,
same man, nearly, with a trout
(and happier days). i ask him
the best ways to fish, and he lets me
lay him down

as i turn to go, he grabs my arm
(and i my pager, just in case) but
his eyes are soft and only honest:
"you're the most beautiful girl
i've ever seen. i love you."

i laugh, blush, tell him goodnight,
and turn out the light

i never see him again.

all this to say, my stay was short,
six months, or so, but still
i have one-thousand tales to break your heart,
even as these people healed my own

(at some point, i stop wishing i would forget you)

heartbreak (a pros & cons list)

pro: you'll start to feel strong, like, really strong, because what other option is there than to keep going? and you've gotta take something from all this, and what doesn't kill you, right?

con: you keep remembering every new day is another one further from the last time you'll ever touch his face, even when—

pro: a real nice fellow from canada will buy you a margarita and listen to you explain too many times why you're wearing a ring. he goes home alone. you go home and don't dream, at least.

con: your seventh-grade fling will ring you up to ask you for a threesome. you'll think about karma for the next few weeks.

pro: people are patient with you, more than you deserve, and you can't say no to such an easy place to rest

con: but their eyes are so sad when they look at you, and they can't help it, but—

pro: you finally understand what all those sad songs really mean when you listen to the radio

con: but god, you wish you didn't

here's the bittersweet twist

i guess you missed me too much to stay gone,
because the next time i saw you, you held me
like you didn't want me to leave

against both our best judgements,
you followed me here (home?)
and we wondered whether we
could be enough, even now

we know better than to make promises.
we'll have to wait & see.

in a highway hotel

i'm not sure when i last looked through a kaleidoscope,
but i imagine it was something just like this,
prism fractals, dizzying, oh-so-pretty
in your eyes, high in your hands, rainbow quilted sheets
and i'd known that when i met you again,
it'd be some wicked conjury, some enchantment
(*this can't be real*) i'm all yours, babe (*this isn't fair*)
until we take this lens away, i'll twirl in these
explosive lights, just as i always used to

heirloom

misfortune runs on my mother's side,
a genetic disposition for disappointment,
short straws, and loving men who don't
deserve such a full-bodied love

for worrying about that which she cannot change
and not changing that which she could
but for fear of helping herself

stubborn hope runs on my mother's side, too
like the dimples of an impossible smile and
a resistance to the way the world works
when there's only climb and clamor left

for there is always something to laugh about,
a song to dance with, all the better if it's
only your own

luck of the irish

is unwanted kisses,
is invasions, is famine,
is whiskey and
a shot of optimism

it's keeping your
chin up and fists clenched,
is a quick dance,
is a loud laugh,

is finding my gold mine
in the west, is chasing
rainbows, is clovers and
cheer and the good fight fought

a self-care mantra

h$_2$o (two liters), eight-thousand meters,
and feed that body well;

homemade face mask, steam-hot bubble bath
and clean up where you dwell;

take a nap, close your tired eyes, unwrap,
and negative thoughts dispel;

inhale, exhale, remember it's alright to fail,
and that the try-again will tell;

to yourself be kind, happy state of mind
and care for every cell;

that time we tried again

you likely won't remember, but,
that night in the bed that was
neither yours nor mine,
a white-flag rendezvous where we
didn't dare to guess the future,
when our dogs slept by our feet
and you slipped your hand in mine,
i rested my head against your side—

if every night could be the same,
i'd take it. i don't care that we
couldn't look each other in the eyes,
i'd close them and listen to you breathe,
well, that would be enough for me.

cardiac

i can taste *my heart* like saltwater
in the back of my mouth, like a
hummingbird caught in my throat,
like i learned to swallow my pride
but not the shame or fear or, you
know, any other feeling. *my heart*
has instinct, *my heart* knows
one-thousand-and-one ways to die,
my heart protects itself with costal
affairs but never lies and still likes
to vacation to my sleeve. *my heart*,
you know, is fine how it is, cautious
but hospitable and healing and here.

naturally disastrous

me: a hurricane, but shy
in a way that doesn't suit storms
where all is calm but the eyes

and i have been called too kind
where i drip naivety and trust
like a leaky faucet and one day,
girl, one day the real world is
gonna get you—
as if
my sweetness is a shortcoming,
my decency a death sentence
in a world somehow more real
than the one i've been living in
for the past twenty years—
no
like yellowstone,
we choose either to be good or
to be destructive, and there are
enough real world hurricanes
for me to stay at sea

we always felt the same

could you look at me again, my dear,
the way you always did,
with your eyes upturned & light
adoration in your grin

could you forgive a sin so sad
& forget your cracking ribs,
breathe us back to life as if
this hurt had never been

could you be so foolish,
could you be so kind,
could we come back from this?

one kiss at a time, my dear,
one day, one breath, one year. . .
i cannot say i love you (yet)
but i'm happy that you're here

confessions of a windy day

everyone says that, if not for me,
the weather would be perfect,

that i tousle hair and chill bones
and am at my best as a breeze,
a mere whisper of myself,
only sought as i hold back

but all i've ever yearned to do
is blow the world away

i think i just love too harshly
and if you felt the way i did,
you'd run fast too

mountain-top dance

it's
a ritual
of mine, upon
reaching the summit,
to outstretch my arms and
shout nonsense joy. i am tired,
but not too tired for a dance, and
the whole world can hear it—at least,
i think they can. i'll sleep well tonight, for once.

anthem of american adoration

you give me fireworks, okay, like, also,
it might be gunshots. i don't know.
only one is illegal here. that's too political.
start again.
you give me fireworks!
i'm terrified of fireworks!
but like all things i'm terrified of,
i'll become captivated in overcoming,
like heights, or spiders, or
rainbow thunder-clap explosions,
or you

yeah, i'll overcome you,
an entire british army, casual colonialism,
unfair fights and boy, you think you've
got me in your empire but
i'm about to george washington your ass

uh,
what i'm really saying is
i don't think we can just be friends,
because i'm capitalism,
i'm all or nothing, billion or bust,
build your dreams in my hands
and i'll give you breadcrumbs
to bake with

i'm democracy,
i'll let you choose your own adventure
as long as your adventure leads to me
and then i'll just declare my independence,

okay, because you pursue property
and i pursue happiness

i need so much from you and
you give me so much i don't need.
we are a country of bountiful bullshit,
you and i, quarreling patriots,
bipartisan babbling, juxtaposed,
at-odds diversity and
baby, all we do is argue

but, like, really,
you're better than the rest,
my favorite challenge,
my hard-to-love homeland
so, for you, i'll watch the fireworks,
let them light up my eyes like
the impossible dream,
my destiny manifest

leg day

how sweet the ache in my legs
the day after pushing myself
to run a little further, to breathe
a little harder. the mirror smiles
back this time, satisfied & sore,
ready for more

i tell the same to my heart.
this ache is something to proud of,
for meeting the challenge of
such a hellbent love. dear,
it isn't broken, just healing
and, like any other muscle,
will be stronger for it

on education:

is confidence.
is the challenge which eases itself.
is turning straw to gold.
is privilege.
is fighting that fear of the unknown.
is power.
is bliss.
is potential.
is telling myself i am able.
is the sky opening up its locked doors.
is the earth whispering her secrets.
is discovery.
is life.

disobedience

ask anyone—i've never failed
at being a good girl, boy,
until it came to you

born into quiet and conformity,
shyness and submission
do-anything to please-anyone
bruised will, broken knees,
candy cane spine

until you showed me the joy to disobey,
you know the ways
you taught me a curved backbone
worked just as well for bad behavior

i mean, you and me?
we've always been made to mutiny
hearts a riot against any sense,
illiterate sinners, led blind to
transgression by temptation
which we never tried to resist

it's no wonder i keep coming back to you.
everyone has called me a fool,
and i could bend over backward for them,
or i could do it my own way for you

chemistry

i keep my class notes clean—
bullet-points, high-lights,
easy to read for late nights
but chemistry is messy,
illegible, not that i could
understand otherwise,
margins filled with
question marks & distracted doodles,
triple-underlined equations that
have pooled in my brain like alphabet soup.
chemistry is messy.
potential energy & breaking bonds
& molecular geometry—
as if i could touch something so
small and all-mighty, like i
could rest in universal existence &
dare to understand divinity &
the world melted away in
seven days of eternal entropy
& chemistry is messy,
for how he pushed & i pulled &
poles reversed & i was brought to my knees
by the attraction which dragged me down,
the density dropping to my gut
& the vacuum in my chest.
some molecules are unstable
when they are alone,
so i could be some diatomic disaster
without something to hold me back
but then, with all this potential,
catch me combusting, watch me explode

dark affairs

she carries me, the night, within her dark womb,
the softest lover, a midnight matinee,
having heard my quiet whispers wanting
more than any man before,
she cradles me in gentle rapture
she stands guard outside my door
from where the television mumbles,
glowing, restless, humming, mad
she blocks the cracks that always open
she listens when i ask for more
and as these inhibitions go,
i turn and toss in fevered dreams
i am alone, but am i lonely?
i'll only let her see

april (ii)

you didn't make a fool of me, april,
not this year.

i put out buckets to collect your rain
and melancholy

and planted pink flowers with it.

dear april,

i think i fell in love again, or i remembered
how a smile tastes

and wings tickled my chest as the sun
called me close

the winter is over, sweet april,
i thawed out my hope,
warmth in my cheeks,

and i'm almost there, dear april.
i'm almost there.

garden of gods

we walked amongst those bloodshot monoliths,
silent (what was there left to say?)

but i did think:
what if we got lost here, could we trust
in far-off stars, or would we spend
the night in wild dark, would you
hold me to the end?
if an earthquake came and toppled
these stones, would we make it
out as one, would we run for our
own lives, would you leave me
behind—or would we be buried
in some hallowed grave, always
side-by-side?
or if the gods themselves looked
down on us, plucked us up like
weeds, would you obey divinity,
or would you beg and plead
to stay with me, could we defy
what's meant to be?

i looked at you. i wondered if you
overthought such things too.
who knows, but you did smile a little
and took my hand in yours.

how bad could it really be,
to sleep under those stars?

mercy

love me merciful
(like so)

cradle me vulnerable
(be soft)

fill me with that
second-chance revival,
that two-toned forgiveness
(like so)

h & k

this has been the hardest to put into words.

i was never alone with you two, really,
which was some saving grace.

if i could have just one more day,
i'd take you to the woods
and we would run, but all i have here
is a decayed shame that i should have
fought harder for you.

it's been over a year,
and the knot in my chest still
tightens when i think of you,
daily, probably, and it
never gets better. i miss you.

of everything that's happened,
i am the most sorry for this—
sweet things, always there for me,
and i couldn't be the same.

you were the best of them.

one step forward...

i thought forgiveness would be easy
a closed-fence decision,
a sign-on-the-dotted-line one-and-done deal

but honestly, sometimes when i'm kissing you
i'll remember where your lips have been

at this point, it's pretty self-destructive,
masochism at best, and i make the mistake
of wishing things might return to how
they were before—
but where did that path lead us?

one day i'll learn this new religion,
stop searching for old-world stars that
were lost in supernovas. tonight,
my knees just feel too weak.

the day i resolved to forget yesterday;

ignore tomorrow,
daises sprouted from my
chest like a new life like
a daybreak like
that first exhale since
the first inhale &
right now is my goal;
today is clotheslined to
all that i am &
i am the wind & sun & a
forgery of all that i conjure;
i close the door on all else;
i live today.
i live today.

hey, may

tell me more about tomorrow
how the warm days went

for now, you'll do, just
fresh-inked bucket lists,
loose strings trimmed neat,
a little hope, a little despair,
and all the sweet flowers,
not quite so thirsty yet

revelations

i am stronger than i believe;
after everything, i should
know that. i could make
it through end of days,
with soot on my forehead,
limping, gasping for breath,
and alive.

i am persephone. i am my
mother's daughter. i am a
survivor from the start,
no one can take away my spirit
without my sacred permission
and i am not here to give it up.

there are few things more frightfully
enduring than a girl who has
learned to cope.

tidal lock

(in which you are the earth, and i am the moon)

i. lunar eclipse
you are all cliffsides and oceans,
inescapable and whole while
i am small and made of craters

but i have my own hold on you,
one part gravity, another part mystic,
and even when you cast your
shadows all over me, i set them aflame
for you to revel in

ii. solar eclipse
i am no innocent, either,
for all the times i've stolen your sun
cursed your sky with burning rings

there is no getting away from each other.
you and i, we were born from collision
and disaster, we are predestined and permanent
but mostly, we are alone, besides one another,
so for all our celestial calamity,
i'll stay beside you, revolving together

storm warning

looks like lightning tonight, boys,
with that fifty-fifty looks-pretty-
while-she-goes-mad coming
from the clouds, spun like
cotton candy by the wind

the lows are in the sub-zeros,
the sub-buried in blankets of
white and down and saved from
the chill of ice,

but the highs are wildfire, a
vesuvius passion that burns
away the rain—expect it all
from this storm, and for the
post hoc prisms

rebirth

i feel i might be whole again,
or, now,
like i might be more of myself
than the old me, or,
the same me with the better skin
and the laugh that is so loud that
those who say it is too loud
cannot be heard

i am the acorn of forgetful squirrels,
i am the yellow weed in the sidewalk cracks,
and i am the stubborn child that insists
it is still a flower

and any spite and regret i clung to
has been lost in the same breeze that
turned my face toward the sun

it is summer;
i am light

p.n.w.

the campfire lights up your eyes
like burgundy gemstones,
your laughter hoarse from
smoke or overuse, i'm not sure

stars brighter than the day you asked,
shall we? and we thought, *why not?*
a born-long-ago dream to see these trees,
and darling, they do not disappoint

home is a little car and one tight tent,
but it's room enough for three
i'll stay here forever, i think,
alive & oregon free

tonight, we'll drink ashy chai
and tell the embers our secrets.
we've been in the woods for five days now,
but tomorrow is the ocean—
i knew she'd wait for us

summit

i gave my legs to the mountains
& wondered if this was this hill i would die on

my neck craned to my back & the peak still
blurred by clouds and hid in hope

wind-tested, endured, burning, fighting,
heaving as rocks threatened avalanche
under my unsteady feet

keep going, keep going,
there is an end to all, and
not even everest is infinite

was it the thin air that stole my breath—
or the hours of exhaustion—
or the god's-eye view?

& look back
look up
point, and say
i was there
i made it

new age dreams

we all grow up being told that we can be
as far as we can imagine—well, small girl, big dreams,
i wanted to be an explorer
fearless in the face of all unknown worlds,
like in the books i'd read by flashlight after bedtime.
someone great, someone brave, someone big
enough to write their name across the skies

then you grow up and you learn the world
has limits and there's nothing left to discover
and dark places are scarier than you thought they'd be.
it's hard to be fearless when all the unknowns
are ugly and better left alone
i'd have made a terrible explorer, anyway,
cause i can't even find home

well i grew up and i saw the world
was ready to be unfolded, and these hands
did belong to an explorer
for dreams are found in valleys and whispers,
late, quiet nights and one day, one day…

so you slow down and learn how to see
with your eyes closed—well, small girl, small dreams,
one day you'll find that one thousand footprints
don't dull the ground and clear skies are meant
for stargazing. little never meant low,
and there's plenty left to seek

san francisco sourdough

my mother always told me,
"you ain't tried real bread
'til you've been to california"
(she was right, of course)

a city built of hills & piers
was waiting for me all these years
had i been whole before?
it's hard to say, but the
ocean always has its way

my father pointed out the bridge,
and it was me—red but golden
all the same, as i looked in wonder
at the blue & brilliant bay

what better place to find your heart
than where people always leave their own?

moving (back) in

this house is smaller than our last
but i don't mind, see,
a new beginning fits here perfectly

neutral ground for us to lay
our worries down—and the
world asked why we're doing this

well, i don't really have a clue,
but if we didn't try again, then
could we say we tried at all?

sweet-heart

i've been called *too nice* too many times,
which is the *nice* way of putting it—
too timid, too weak, too soft-in-the-bones,
too peaceful, passive, pathetic, powerless
it might be my favorite thing about me

i'd rather be so recklessly kind that
my chest aches from the sweetness
than to be no better-off and bitter

flower-garden glasses are the way to grow,
i'll hold the hopeless, i'll kiss the snow

somebody new

you're someone different now,
grown up, smile less but deeper,
calmer after stormy seas and
when i hold your face in my wary palms,
it belongs to a beautiful stranger
who scrapes the crevice of yesterday's dreams

so hold me like you've never known me
never known how it felt to lose me
join me for an easy evening, exploration,
drifters in this brand-new bed,
wanderers who have never met

foreigner, you are welcome here,
lips familiar but not the same, no,
you, boy, you are someone new
yes, i can fall in love with you

dear flat earth society:

pseudoscience is not a way to think
but makes the loveliest metaphors

so, thank you

thank you for making me think about
the edges of the earth,
for turning me toward the horizon,
for standing me on my tiptoes so
that i can scrape the stars

you are no adventurer

you'd seen half the world before you were twenty,
and now, you want a quiet future, made of
slow mornings, closed windows, and home videos

but my shoulders were made
for backpacks and sunburns
see, i spent my first twenty years
too afraid to step outside
but now? i'm ready to go cross oceans, fly to pluto,
i haven't seen nearly enough (who has? you have)
to satisfy these wandering genes

but that's alright, dear.
no need to lie to me
i've grown too fond of being lonely
and the trees make such sweet company.
stay here, make me a bed to fall into
every time my legs need a little rest

it's your turn to wait

a little Faith

for all my doubt,
my need to define existence with boxes and law,
trust in reasonable explanations for the inexplicable,
a nihilist, a skeptic, a scientist at best

i still believe there is magic in the stars
at least, or even a little closer than we see,
which rests in grief, in strength,
in untrimmed grass & white butterflies

i feel it in a soft day's sun rays
warm across my eyelids,
a sweet whisper from the creek bed,
the breath from my own lungs

a patient, perpetual reminder to myself:
a little faith goes the whole way home.

oasis

i'd take you over coffee any day
(and you know how i enjoy my lattes)

see, i'd take you fully clothed,
naked tongues only, laid bare minds
until the rest inevitably follows, well,
you kept me up last night (like coffee)
love, sometimes i am thirsty and you are a desert
but i swear i can drink moonlight as it dances on sand
even when i dream of coral beds
i think i could swallow an entire ocean,
which is a big claim, coming from a girl who never
sleeps

anyway, i'm tongue-tied and tired and
it's warm in these blushing rays, so i'll stay sleepy,
my coffee will grow cold and i'll keep dreaming

turtle dove

if i were a bird,
i would be a turtle—
the world-carrying sort

sea-wings swimming in
some blue galaxy passing
me by

as we children perch paper ship
hats on each other, for
the world is so young

to the caring indifference
of the pantheistic
turtle

this body

this body—is whole
and this body—is full
of the good stuff, that is,
the good life, like i know
how to smile contagious,
and these arms are weak
but they still hug too tight
and my feet are loyal as
my lungs. and i'd like to
feel beautiful, but it's just
as well to feel kind. and
this body—is affectionate
to a fault, is open-palmed
hands, is mild, is made of
chemicals and compassion

impression, sunset

a seashell riverbank lights up my toes
while we watch the sun make her bed
in the folds of the mountains and turn
out the light. i wonder if it is possible
to kiss the stars from the trees, because
i am an entire forest, and you keep my
nights bright. i am in love with the way
i can close my eyes and still see you, &
the sun lets us be

where hope lay

as for the future, i cannot say,
we're still healing, to this day

but even if tomorrow witnessed
us becoming done and distant

i would not regret a single moment
my heart is yours, and even broken—

it would still be worth it, love.
it never stopped. it always was.

acknowledgements

this collection has been, to date, one of my most personal and difficult to write. i have so many to thank, not just for the help in writing this book, but for how these people revived me when i thought there was nothing left.

my family, namely, my mom, dad, grandma, nana, and little brothers.

my friends, especially gwen, rachel, rebekah, jenny, sydnee, tammy, and angie.

mitch, of course, my inspiration in many more ways than one.

and to my readers, always, for being so gentle with these words.

thank you, thank you, thank you.

about the author

bella ryan began writing when she was eight years old, beginning with poetry and progressing to short stories and novels in her early teen years. she wrote and self-published her first book, *sanguine moon*, in 2013. *the reckless kind* is her sixth published work and the follow-up to *sweet hearts*, her debut poetry collection.

when not writing, she might be caught baking, star-gazing, getting lost in the woods, painting, or drinking coffee with too much creamer. she is majoring in biology at u.c.c.s., class of 2021. read more about the poetess and her other work at:

http://isabellarogge.wixsite.com/isabellarogge

Manufactured by Amazon.ca
Bolton, ON

13710499R00052

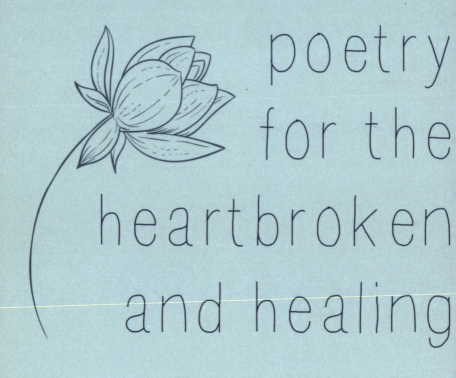

poetry
for the
heartbroken
and healing

ISBN 9798651725113

9 798651 725113

Manufactured by Amazon.ca
Acheson, AB